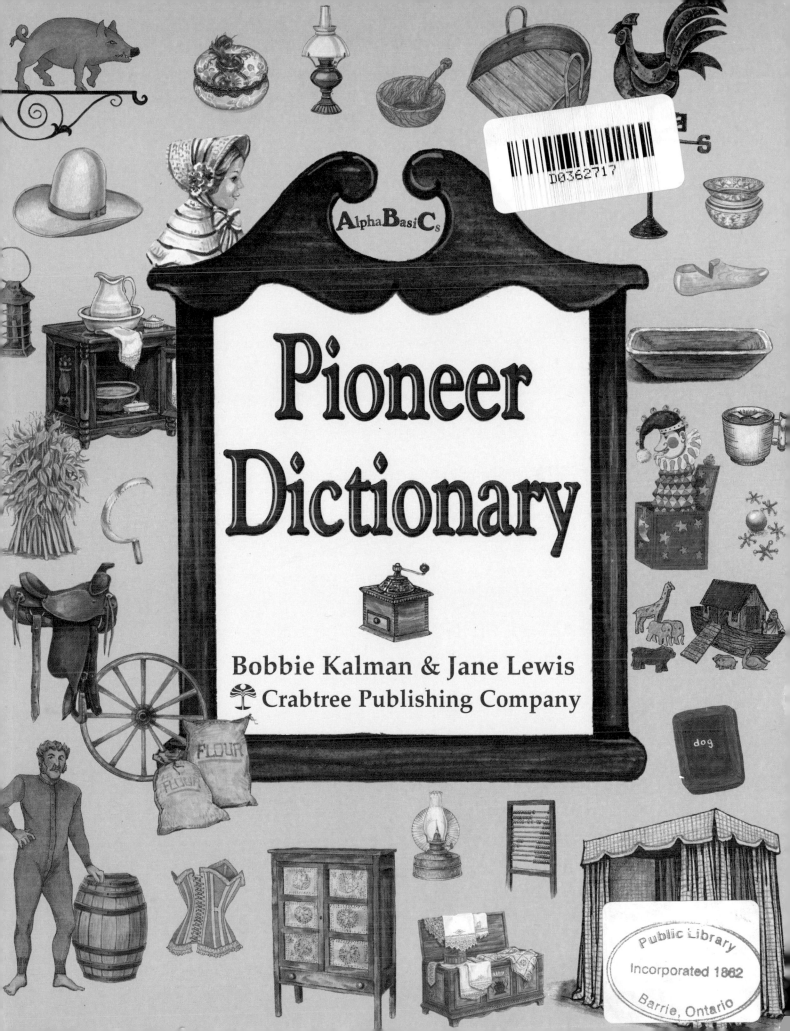

AlphaBasiCs

Pioneer Dictionary

Bobbie Kalman & Jane Lewis
Crabtree Publishing Company

AlphaBasiCs

Created by Bobbie Kalman

To Andrew Lewis, who is defining himself

Editor-in-Chief
Bobbie Kalman

Writing team
Bobbie Kalman
Jane Lewis

Managing editor
Lynda Hale

Editing team
Hannelore Sotzek
Heather Levigne
Kate Calder

Computer design
Jane Lewis
Lynda Hale
John Crossingham (digital enhancing)

Production coordinator
Hannelore Sotzek

Special thanks to
Genessee Country Museum, Brian Adamson, Black Creek Pioneer Village, Colonial Williamsburg Foundation, Sutter's Fort State Historic Park, Fort George National Historic Park

Photographs
Jim Bryant: page 31 (bottom); Marc Crabtree: pages 10, 13, 27 (top), 32 (middle); Peter Crabtree: page 11; Digital Stock: page 17; Eyewire, Inc.: pages 12, 17, 27 (bottom), 29, 32 (left); Ken Faris: pages 19 (top), 32 (right); Bobbie Kalman: pages 5, 14 (top & bottom), 19 (bottom left), 23, 31 (top); Bob Mansour: page 16; Black Creek Pioneer Village, Toronto (T.R.C.A.): pages 3, 22; Tony & Alba Sanches-Zinnanti: page 19 (bottom right)

Illustrations
Barbara Bedell, Halina Below, Antoinette "Cookie" Bortolon, Nancy Cook, Tammy Everts, Eyewire, Inc., Janet Kimantas, Trevor Morgan, Sarah Pallek, Bonna Rouse, David Willis

Separations and film
Dot 'n Line Image Inc.

Printer
Worzalla Publishing Company

Crabtree Publishing Company

PMB 16A	360 York Road	73 Lime Walk
350 Fifth Avenue,	RR 4	Headington,
Suite 3308	Niagara-on-the-Lake	Oxford
New York, NY	Ontario, Canada	OX3 7AD
10118	L0S 1J0	United Kingdom

Cataloging in Publication Data
Kalman, Bobbie
  Pioneer dictionary

(AlphaBasiCs)
Includes index.
ISBN 0-86505-390-1 (library bound) ISBN 0-86505-420-7 (pbk.)
This book is an alphabetical listing of words related to life on the North American frontier, from ague and bank barn to wheelwright and zoetrope.

1. Frontier and pioneer life—North America—Dictionaries, Juvenile. 2. English language—North America—Dictionaries, Juvenile. 3. Americanisms—Dictionaries, Juvenile. 4. North America—Social life and customs—Dictionaries, Juvenile. [1. Frontier and pioneer life—Terminology. 2. English language—Terms and phrases. 3. Americanisms.] I. Title. II. Lewis, Jane. III. Series: Kalman, Bobbie. AlphaBasiCs.

E179.5.K354 2000   j973'.03 21   LC 99-038619
                                                                CIP

abacus A frame with wooden beads on metal rods or wires, which settler children used to help them learn arithmetic

adobe (1) Sun-dried clay used by Native Americans and pioneers in the Southwest to build homes; (2) A home built of sun-dried clay

adz, adze An ax used to make a round log square

ague A name for a fever and periods of chills and sweating; also called malaria

almanac A book published every year giving information about many things, including weather, farming, cooking, and health

andiron A metal object used to hold up logs in a fireplace; also called a firedog

anvil A heavy, cast-iron and steel block used by a blacksmith to shape iron

apiary A place for raising and keeping bees

apothecary (1) A person who prepares and sells medicine; a pharmacist; (2) A shop where medicine is sold

apple peeler A gadget used to peel and core apples

apprentice A person who learns a skill by working with an artisan

arithmetic Mathematics

artisan A skilled tradesperson such as a blacksmith or carpenter

auger A tool used to bore holes into wood

awl A small, pointed tool for making holes in wood or leather

ax, axe A tool with a wooden handle and sharp blade used for chopping wood

abacus

adz

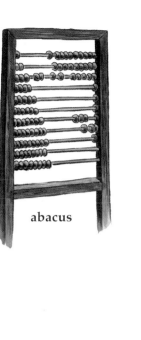

andirons

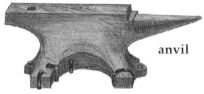

anvil

auger

apothecary (sign)

adobe

awl

apple peeler

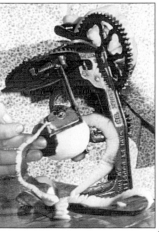

3

bank barn

barrel

basin

bellows

belly warmer

Betty lamp

bloomers

bodice

barn-raising bee

bake kettle *see* dutch oven

bale A tightly bound bundle of hay or wheat

bank barn A barn built into the side of a hill

bannock A type of flatbread made in a frying pan

barn-raising bee An event in which everyone in the community gathers together to build a barn

barrel A large cask that has curved, wooden sides and a flat top and bottom

barter system A system of trading goods and services without using money

basin A large shallow bowl

bayberry A type of berry that is sometimes added to tallow to give candles a pleasant fragrance

bed tick A sack filled with leaves, straw, corn husks, or goose feathers and used as a mattress

bee A work party at which several people in a community come together to do a job, such as building a barn, husking corn, or making a quilt; also called a frolic

bellows A leather bag that pumps out air when squeezed and is used to fan a fire

belly warmer A metal container filled with hot water and used to keep a person warm

benefit A medicine made from herbs

Betty lamp A bowl of animal fat with a wick

blacksmith A person who shapes iron into objects such as horseshoes

bloodletting The medical practice of cutting a person's skin and draining blood from the body, which was thought to cure disease

bloomers Women's loose, baggy trousers that were gathered at the ankle. They were named after Amelia Bloomer, who started the fashion.

boardwalk A sidewalk made of wooden boards

bodice The upper part of a dress

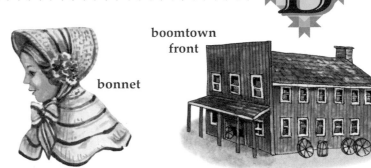

bonnet A woman's hat with ribbons that tie under the chin

boomtown A town that grows quickly in population

boomtown front A square false storefront built to make a building appear larger and the business more prosperous

boot scraper A metal object located outside the home and used for removing dirt from the bottom of boots or shoes

bowler *see* derby

brake An instrument used to crush flax

branding iron An instrument that is heated and then used to burn a brand, or symbol, into an animal's skin to show who owns the animal

bread oven An opening in the side of a fireplace. This oven was used to bake bread, biscuits, and cakes.

bridle A harness made of leather straps that is put on a horse's head in order to control the horse

broadax, broadaxe An ax with a large head and short handle

bronco buster A person who tames wild horses

buckskin A strong, soft leather made from the skin of a male deer

buffalo An oxlike animal that once roamed the Great Plains; also called a bison

buffalo chips Dried buffalo dung that was used as fuel for fires

burlap A coarse cloth woven from the fiber of the jute plant and used to make sacks

bustle A pad or hoop that adds fullness to the back of a skirt

butter churn A container with a dasher used for making butter

butter mold, butter mould A carved, wooden container into which butter was pressed to give it a decorative shape

bonnet

boomtown front
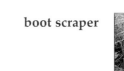

boot scraper

brake

branding iron

bridle

bustle

broadax

bread oven

butter mold

butter churn

buckskin

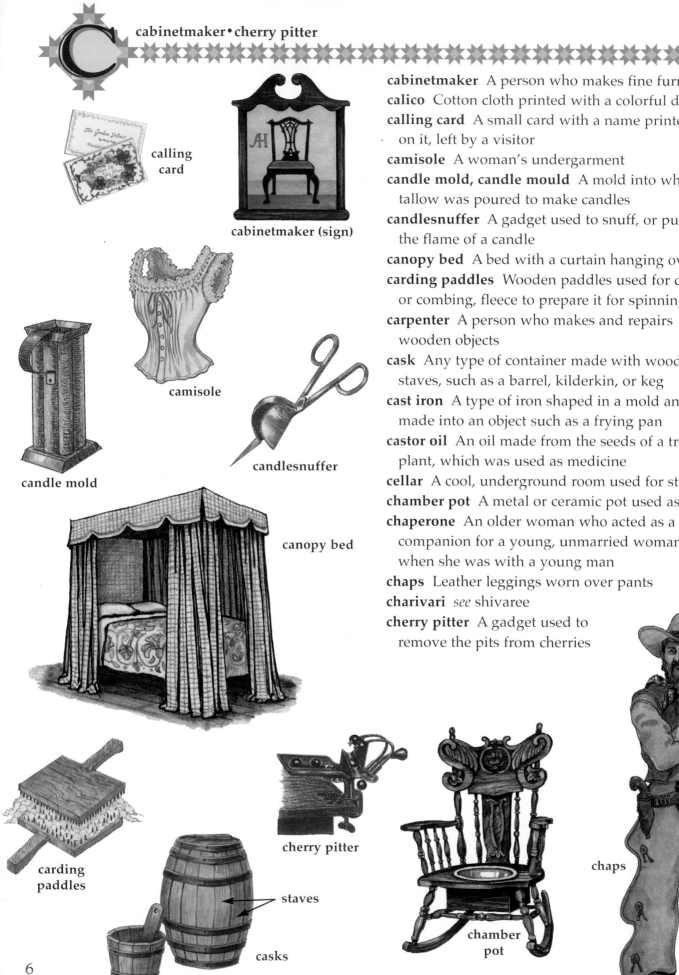

cabinetmaker A person who makes fine furniture

calico Cotton cloth printed with a colorful design

calling card A small card with a name printed on it, left by a visitor

camisole A woman's undergarment

candle mold, candle mould A mold into which tallow was poured to make candles

candlesnuffer A gadget used to snuff, or put out, the flame of a candle

canopy bed A bed with a curtain hanging over it

carding paddles Wooden paddles used for carding, or combing, fleece to prepare it for spinning

carpenter A person who makes and repairs wooden objects

cask Any type of container made with wooden staves, such as a barrel, kilderkin, or keg

cast iron A type of iron shaped in a mold and made into an object such as a frying pan

castor oil An oil made from the seeds of a tropical plant, which was used as medicine

cellar A cool, underground room used for storage

chamber pot A metal or ceramic pot used as a toilet

chaperone An older woman who acted as a companion for a young, unmarried woman when she was with a young man

chaps Leather leggings worn over pants

charivari *see* shivaree

cherry pitter A gadget used to remove the pits from cherries

calling card

cabinetmaker (sign)

camisole

candlesnuffer

candle mold

canopy bed

carding paddles

cherry pitter

staves

casks

chamber pot

chaps

6

chicken coop

chuck wagon

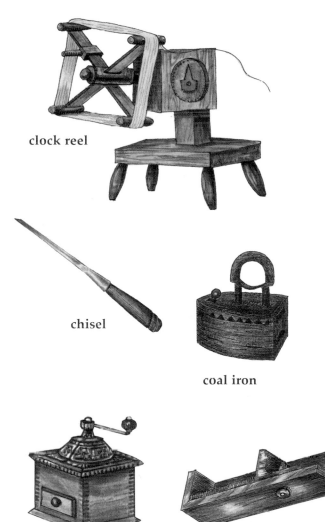

clock reel

chisel

coal iron

coffee grinder

composing stick

chicken coop A small outbuilding in which chickens are kept

chisel A cutting tool with a sharp, angled edge

chuck wagon A wagon that carried food, supplies, and cooking equipment for cowhands

circular A letter to which people added their own news and then mailed on to other family members

claim A piece of land chosen by a miner on which he or she searched for gold

clock reel A gadget used to wind yarn while counting the number of turns so that the user would know when a skein was finished

coal iron A wood-handled metal box filled with hot coals that was used to press wrinkles out of clothing

coffee grinder A gadget used to crush coffee beans

colander A bowl with small holes in the sides and bottom used for draining liquid from foods

composing stick A metal holder on which letters were placed to form words that would then be printed on a printing press

compositor A person who placed letters and characters into a galley at a print shop

consumption An early word for tuberculosis, a disease of the lungs

cooper A person who makes barrels and buckets

copybook A notebook in which schoolchildren practiced their handwriting

corduroy road A road built of logs

corncrib

cornhusk doll

corset

corncrib An outbuilding used for storing corn, usually raised on posts to keep out mice

cornhusk doll A doll made from dried corn husks

cornpone *see* johnny cake

corral A circular fenced area in which horses are kept and trained

corset A stiff undergarment that was laced tightly on a woman's upper body; also called a stay

covered wagon A wagon with a covered top; also called a Conestoga wagon

cradle (1) A scythe with three wooden fingers and a blade; (2) A rocking bed for an infant

craftsperson A person skilled in creating handmade goods

crane A swinging iron bar inside a fireplace, from which pots were hung over the fire

crinoline (1) A petticoat made of stiff fabric; (2) A hooped petticoat

crock A clay or stone jar or pot

cruet A small bottle for storing oil or vinegar

culottes Wide-legged trousers that look like a skirt

cuspidor *see* spittoon

cutler A craftsperson who makes and repairs knives and other objects used for cutting

cutter A small sleigh pulled by one horse

crock

covered wagon

crane

crinoline

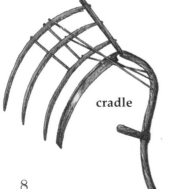

cradle

cutter

8

dasher The stick or plunger inside a butter churn

derby A man's hat with a round crown and narrow brim; also called a bowler

divining rod A forked branch or stick used for finding underground water

dogmill A wooden wheel in which a small dog ran to power a gadget such as a spit or butter churn

dogtrot A roofed outdoor passageway located between two buildings

domestic A household servant or maid

dough box A table with a removable box or trough

draft horse *see* workhorse

drawers Short pants worn as underwear

drawing room *see* parlor

drawknife A blade with handles at both ends, used by woodworkers to shave wood

dry goods Items such as cloth, thread, and ribbon; also called soft goods

dugout A home built into the ground or hillside

dunce cap A cone-shaped hat worn by students as a punishment for not understanding a lesson

dutch oven A large covered pot used for baking bread, rolls, and biscuits; also called a bake kettle

dwelling A place where a person lives; a home

ear trumpet A large metal horn-shaped object used as a hearing aid

embroidery Decorative stitching done on fabric

emigrant A person who leaves his or her home to live in another place

epidemic The sudden spread of disease among many people

dasher / churn / derby

dogmill

dogtrot

drawers / drawknife / dunce cap / dutch oven

ear trumpet

F

fan

fife

felloe

firepan

fireplace

flail

fleece

flatter

fleam

fob

forge

foot stove

frame house

fan An object made of feathers or paper that people wave to keep cool

farrier A person who shoes horses

felloe A curved section of wood that formed part of a wagon-wheel rim

fiddle A type of violin

fife A small flutelike musical instrument

finishing mill A sawmill that produced smooth planks of wood, doors, railings, and wall moldings

fire brigade A group that fights fires

firedog *see* andiron

firepan A long-handled metal pan used for carrying burning coals from one place to another

fireplace A brick or clay structure in which a fire can be built safely

firkin A small barrel often used to hold butter or soap

flail A tool used by farmers to thresh grain, or remove the seeds from the stalks

flapjack A small pancake cooked on a griddle

flatiron A heavy iron that was heated over a fire or stovetop and used to press wrinkled fabric

flatter A hammer used by metalworkers to smooth out the surface of metal; also called a set hammer

flax A plant with thin stems and blue flowers whose fiber is used to make linen cloth

fleam An instrument used for cutting skin in order to draw blood

fleece The wool of a sheep

fob (1) A ribbon or chain attached to a watch; (2) An ornament attached to the end of a watch chain

foot stove A metal box filled with hot coals and kept near the feet to warm the toes

forge A raised fireplace on which a blacksmith works

founder A person who melts different metals together to create new metals and shapes them into objects such as candlesticks

frame house A house built by nailing planks to a frame; also called a plank house

frolic *see* bee

frontier The undeveloped region beyond a settled area

frumenty A porridge made of wheat boiled in milk

G

galley A shallow tray containing letters and characters to be printed on a page

game Wild animals that people hunt

garland A string of vines, flowers, and leaves that are tied together and hung as a decoration

gauntlet A thick leather glove with a long cuff worn to protect the hand and wrist

general store A store selling a wide range of items such as food, cloth, clothing, hardware, tools, and household goods

ghost town The remains of a town that is no longer inhabited by people

goffer A metal roller used to iron the bows and frills on bonnets and collars

gold rush A large migration of people to an area where gold has been discovered

governess A single woman hired by parents to teach and take care of their children

granary A building in which grain is stored

Great Plains A large area of flat, grass-covered land located in central North America

griddle A flat metal pan or surface used for cooking

grindstone A flat stone disk that is turned on an axle to sharpen tools

gristmill A building with machinery that ground grain into flour

gruel A liquid food made by boiling cereal in water or milk

gunny sack A large burlap bag used for holding goods such as sugar, spices, or vegetables

gunsmith A person who makes and repairs guns

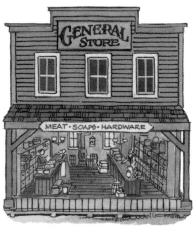
garland

gauntlet

general store

goffer

griddle

grindstone

gunsmith (sign)

gunny sack

gristmill

11

H

handcart

hair receiver

harness

harpsichord

harrow

hatchel

hayfork

hay knife

Hereford

hitching post

hair receiver A fancy dish used to hold hair with which pioneers made jewelry

handcart A wooden cart pulled by a person instead of an animal

harness The straps connecting a horse to a carriage

harness maker A leatherworker who makes saddles and harnesses for horses

harpsichord A musical instrument similar to a piano

harrow A heavy wooden farm tool with spikes, used to break up soil

hatchel A wooden instrument with steel teeth, used for combing flax to make it ready for weaving

hatter A person who makes, sells, and repairs hats

hay Grass, clover, or other plants that have been cut and dried for animal feed

hay burner A stove that burned hay as fuel

hayfork A long-handled wooden tool with sharp prongs, used to gather straw and hay

hay knife A two-handled knife used to cut chunks of hay from a pile

hearth A fireplace floor made of brick or stone

heifer A young cow that has not yet given birth

hemp A tall plant whose stem contains fibers used for making string and rope

herb A plant used to make medicine or to flavor food

Hereford A type of cattle with a red-colored coat that has white markings

hide The skin of an animal

hitching post A wooden frame located outside a building, to which horses were tied

hod *see* scuttle

hogshead A large barrel

12

homespun Plain handmade wool fabric

homestead All the land and buildings that form a person's property

homesteader A person who owns a homestead

hominy A hot cereal made of coarsely ground kernels of corn boiled in milk or water

hoop A wooden or iron ring often used as a toy

hoop

hope chest A chest used by a young woman to collect fine linens and household items in preparation for marriage and keeping a home of her own

hornbook A wooden paddle on which a piece of paper showing letters, numbers, and Bible verses was protected by a thin, transparent layer of horn

hornbook

housewarming A celebration held in the house into which a family has recently moved

hub The center of a wagon wheel

husk The dry outer covering of certain fruits or seeds such as that surrounding an ear of corn

icehouse A small building with a hole in the floor for holding chunks of ice, which kept the building cool for storing food

illumination The art of painting or decorating a page or the first letter of a page in a book

immigrant A person who comes to live in a place that is far from where he or she was born

India ink A thick black ink used in drawing

indigo A plant used to make blue dye

inkwell A small container that holds ink for writing

iron horse A railroad steam engine or locomotive

itinerant An artisan who traveled from place to place with his or her tools, living with and working for one family after another

hope chest

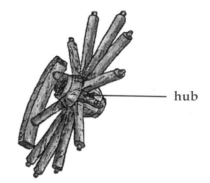

hub

illumination

inkwell

iron horse

13

jack

jack bed

Jacob's ladder

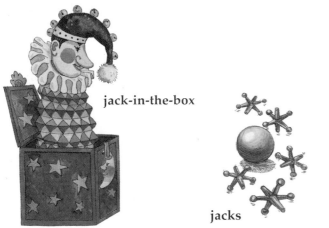
jack-in-the-box

jacks

jack (1) A gadget used to turn a spit above a fire; (2) A worker, such as a lumberjack

jack bed A bed that was built into a log house when the house was constructed

jack-in-the-box A decorated toy box with a crank on one side that, on turning, causes an object to pop out of the box

jacks A popular children's game using small metal objects called jacks and a rubber ball

jackstraws A popular game in which splinters or straws are heaped on a table, and players pull out straws, trying not to move the rest of the pile

Jacob's ladder A toy made of several flat blocks connected with ribbon, which appeared to flip down when held in the air

jerky Meat that is dried over a fire so it does not spoil

jig A fast hopping dance

johnny cake A flat cake made of cornmeal and cooked in a pan; also called cornpone

journal A book used for writing daily thoughts or events; a diary

journeyman A trained artisan who did not have his or her own shop but worked for another craftsperson

jig

kaleidoscope A moveable tube containing mirrors and pieces of colored glass that create beautiful patterns inside the tube

keelboat A boat that was used for transporting goods on a river

keg A small strong barrel

kerosene, kerosine A type of oil used to light lamps

kerosene lamp A lamp fueled by kerosene

kettle A pot used for boiling water

kilderkin A cask that can hold half as much liquid as a barrel

kiln (1) An oven made of bricks used for firing, or baking, clay to make pottery; (2) An oven used for baking or drying grain

kilt A knee-length pleated skirt traditionally worn by Scottish boys and men

kindling Dry twigs or small pieces of wood used to start fires

knickerbockers Short pants that extend just below the knees; also called knickers

knickers *see* knickerbockers

kaleidoscope

keelboat

kettle

kilt

knickerbockers

kerosene lamp

15

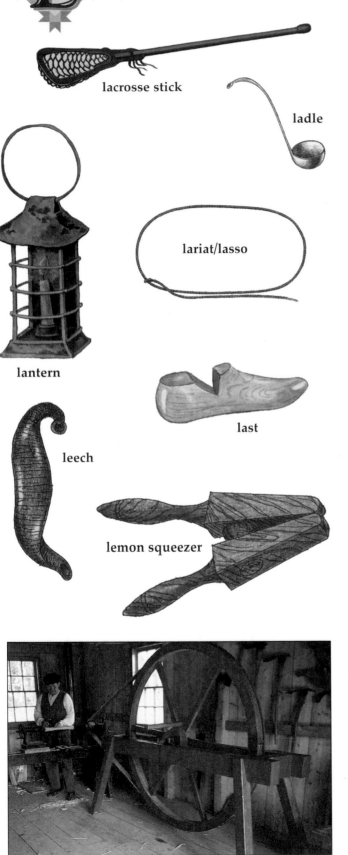

lacrosse stick

ladle

lantern

lariat/lasso

last

leech

lemon squeezer

lathe

lacrosse A field game in which two teams use sticks with nets to catch and throw a rubber ball; originally a Native North American game

ladle A large spoon used to serve liquid, such as soup

lantern A case that holds a light source, such as a candle, and allows light to shine through its sides

lanthorn Another word for lantern

lard Pork fat

lariat A rope used to catch animals; also called a lasso

last Hand-carved, foot-shaped blocks of wood used by a shoemaker to make or repair shoes

latch A mechanism, usually a small bar fitted into a notch, that connects a closed door to a door frame or a gate to a fence

latchstring A small string on the outside of a door that, when pulled, releases the latch and opens a door or gate

lathe A machine used by cabinetmakers to shape wood

lean-to A rough shelter with three walls, one of which is the sloped roof that reaches the ground

leatherworker A person who makes leather items such as saddles or shoes

leech A worm that sucks blood from other animals; it was used by doctors to draw blood from patients as a medical treatment

lemon squeezer A wooden press used to squeeze the juice out of a lemon

lightning rod A metal pole attached to the roof of a building. During a storm, lightning hits the rod and travels down through a wire into the ground, instead of hitting the wooden building and starting a fire. Some lightning rods had glass balls attached. If the glass cracked, it meant the building had been struck by lightning.

linen Cloth made from flax fibers

linsey-woolsey Cloth made of linen and wool

lightning rod

16

loft

livestock

log house

longhorn

livestock The animals kept on a farm, such as horses, cattle, oxen, chickens, pigs, and sheep

locust A large grasshopper that travels in a group called a swarm

lode A deposit of gold or other metals in the earth

loft A flat, open area built underneath the roof of a house or barn

logger *see* lumberjack

log house A type of home built in wooded areas with walls made from large logs

longhorn A type of cattle with very long horns

loom A machine used to weave yarn or thread into cloth

love apple A tomato

lugpole A wooden pole that was used to support a kettle or pot over a fire

lumber Any wood that has been sawed into large boards or planks

lumberjack A person who cuts down trees and transports them to a sawmill; also called a logger

lute A guitar-like musical instrument

lye A strong, liquid chemical made by pouring water over wood ashes that was used to make soap

lugpole

loom

lute

17

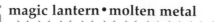

magic lantern

mezzaluna

milk jug

millinery (sign)

mill pick

millstone

millrace

moccasins

mold

magic lantern An early type of slide projector

mallet A hammer with a wooden head

manger A wooden trough used for feeding cattle or horses

maple sugar Sugar made from maple sap

mason A craftsperson who works with stone, bricks, or concrete

merchant A storekeeper

mezzaluna A curved knife used to chop vegetables

midwife A woman who assists pregnant women in childbirth

milk jug A large metal can used to hold milk

mill A building with machines, such as a sawmill, that turns raw materials into a finished product

milldam A dam built to hold back water in order to form a millpond

miller A person who runs a mill

milliner A person who makes and sells women's hats

millinery A women's hat shop

mill pick A tool used to cut grooves, or furrows, into a millstone

millpond A pond located near a mill, used to contain water for powering the mill's water wheel

millrace The channel through which water flows from the millpond to the water wheel; also called a millrun

millrun *see* millrace

millstone A large, round stone used for grinding grain in a gristmill

mincemeat A mixture of chopped apples, raisins, spices, and meat that is used as pastry filling

miner A person who digs in the ground in search of precious metals such as gold or silver

mission A religious settlement in which priests attempt to convert people to Christianity

moccasins Soft leather shoes without heels, originally worn by Native Americans

molasses A thick, dark syrup made from raw sugar; also called treacle

mold, mould A hollow container into which hot fluid material such as molten metal is poured so that when the fluid cools and hardens, it will take on the shape of the container

molten metal Any metal that has been heated to become liquid

MNO

monster wheel *see* walking wheel

mortar (1) A substance such as clay, mud, moss, or wood chips used to fill the spaces between the logs of a log cabin; (2) A wooden bowl in which grains or spices are crushed with a pestle

mourning pin A brooch containing a piece of hair from a deceased family member

mouser A cat that hunts mice and rats

mow The area in a barn where hay and straw are stored

muff A warm tubelike covering for the hands

muley saw A type of saw used in early sawmills to cut logs into planks

mustache cup, moustache cup A cup with a ledge that protected a man's mustache from getting wet while drinking

Native Americans Aboriginal peoples of North America

needlepoint A craft in which designs are stitched onto cloth using a diagonal stitch

needlework A handicraft, such as sewing or embroidery, that is done with a needle

niddy-noddy A wooden gadget used to wind yarn into a skein by hand

Noah's Ark toy A small wooden model of Noah's Ark and pairs of animals modeled after the Biblical story

noggin A wooden cup

nutmeg A fragrant tropical seed that is ground into a powder and used as a spice

nutmeg grater A gadget used to grate nutmeg

oil lamp A lamp made from a wick dipped in oil

one-room school A school building in which all the children were taught in one room by one teacher

open range A large area of grazing land

outbuilding A small building on a farm, such as an outhouse, that was set apart from the main house and barn

outdoor oven An oven built outside the house that was used for baking bread and pastry

outhouse An outdoor toilet; also called a privy

ox cart A small wagon pulled by oxen

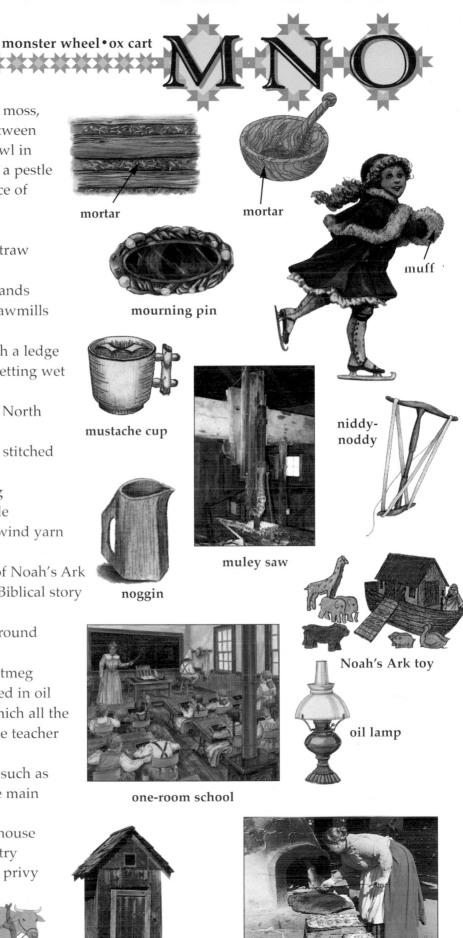

mortar

mortar

mourning pin

muff

mustache cup

niddy-noddy

muley saw

noggin

Noah's Ark toy

oil lamp

one-room school

ox cart

outhouse

outdoor oven

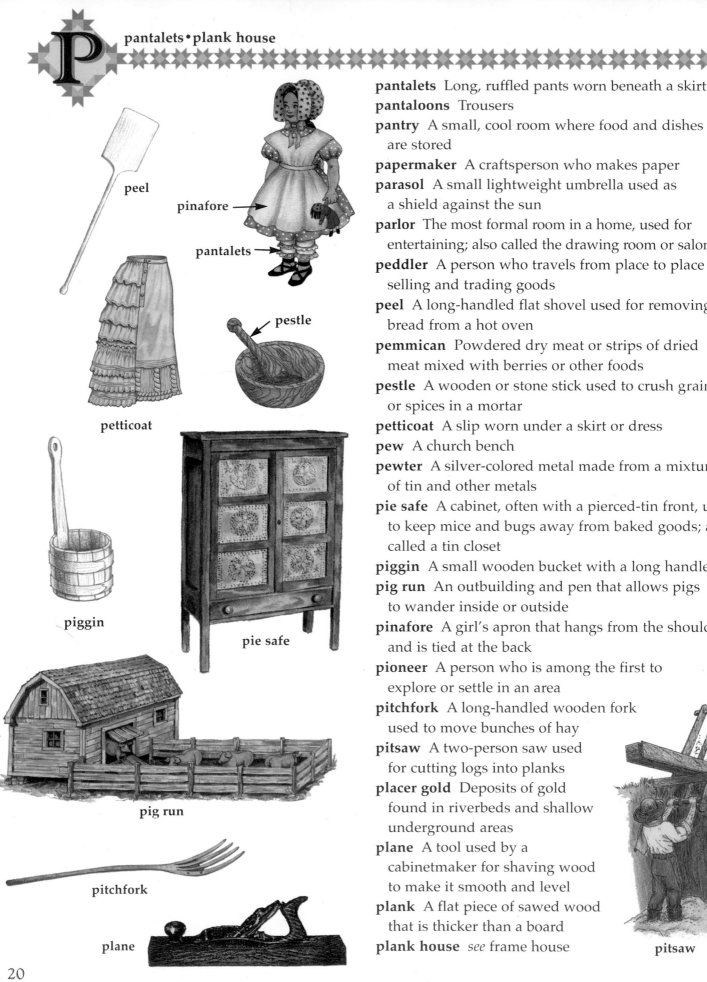

peel

pinafore

pantalets

pestle

petticoat

piggin

pie safe

pig run

pitchfork

plane

pitsaw

pantalets Long, ruffled pants worn beneath a skirt

pantaloons Trousers

pantry A small, cool room where food and dishes are stored

papermaker A craftsperson who makes paper

parasol A small lightweight umbrella used as a shield against the sun

parlor The most formal room in a home, used for entertaining; also called the drawing room or salon

peddler A person who travels from place to place selling and trading goods

peel A long-handled flat shovel used for removing bread from a hot oven

pemmican Powdered dry meat or strips of dried meat mixed with berries or other foods

pestle A wooden or stone stick used to crush grain or spices in a mortar

petticoat A slip worn under a skirt or dress

pew A church bench

pewter A silver-colored metal made from a mixture of tin and other metals

pie safe A cabinet, often with a pierced-tin front, used to keep mice and bugs away from baked goods; also called a tin closet

piggin A small wooden bucket with a long handle

pig run An outbuilding and pen that allows pigs to wander inside or outside

pinafore A girl's apron that hangs from the shoulders and is tied at the back

pioneer A person who is among the first to explore or settle in an area

pitchfork A long-handled wooden fork used to move bunches of hay

pitsaw A two-person saw used for cutting logs into planks

placer gold Deposits of gold found in riverbeds and shallow underground areas

plane A tool used by a cabinetmaker for shaving wood to make it smooth and level

plank A flat piece of sawed wood that is thicker than a board

plank house *see* frame house

20

P

plaster A thick paste applied to an area of the body for medicinal purposes

plow A tool used to break up and turn over the soil before planting crops

poke A wooden brace placed around an animal's neck to prevent it from getting through a fence

pomander A fruit covered in cloves and other spices that, when dried, creates a pleasing aroma

porringer A wooden bowl made from a hollowed-out log, used for eating soup or porridge

potash A substance made by boiling away the water from lye and used for making soap

potato boiler A wire basket used to hold potatoes while they boiled inside a larger pot. When the basket was removed from the pot, the water drained off the potatoes.

potbellied stove A low, rounded wood-burning stove

potpourri A mixture of dried flowers, fruits, herbs, and spices that is used for fragrance

pottery Items such as cups, bowls, or vases made of clay that has been fired in a kiln

poultice A thick paste applied to a swollen or infected area of the body to take down the swelling or absorb the infection

prairie A vast area of grassland with very few trees

prairie schooner A covered wagon that, with its wooden wagon and canvas cover, looked like a ship from a distance as it crossed the plains

preserves Fruit treated with sugar and stored in bottles to keep it from spoiling; jams and jellies

primer A book containing the alphabet, numbers, and poems used by children learning to read

printer A person who runs a printing press

privy *see* outhouse

produce Farm products such as fruits and vegetables

prospector A person who searches for gold or other valuable metals

pueblo A Native American dwelling made of adobe

puncheon A large log split in half, with the flat side smooth. Puncheons were used to form the floor of a log house.

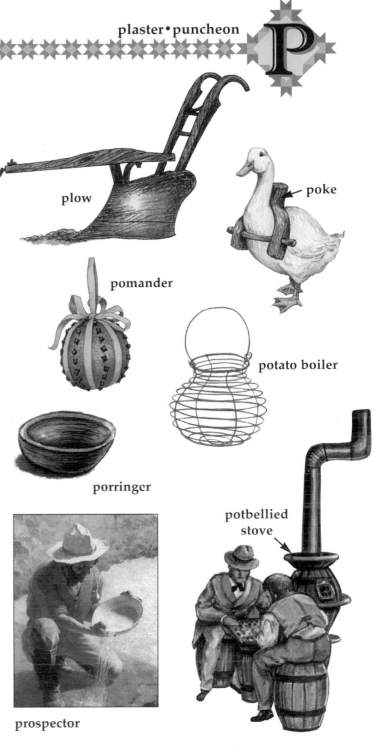

plow

poke

pomander

potato boiler

porringer

prospector

potbellied stove

prairie schooner

puncheons

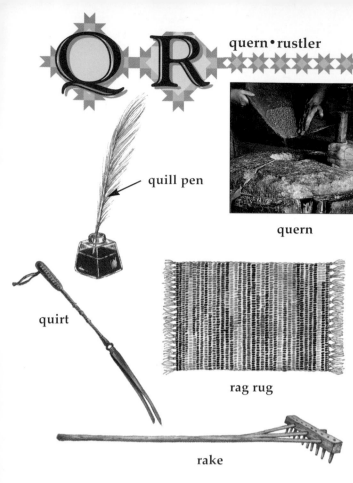

quill pen

quern

quirt

rag rug

rake

ranch

rolling pin

roof tree

rug beater

quern A hand mill with two round, flat stones used for grinding grain

quill pen A pen made from a feather

quilt A blanket made from pieces of fabric sewn into a pattern

quirt A whip used in horse riding

rafter A sloping beam that helps form and support a roof

raftsman A logger who sailed a raft of logs down a river to a sawmill

rag rug A colorful rug made from strips of used clothing and fabric

railhead The end of a railway line

rake A long-handled wooden tool used to gather straw and leaves or to smooth dirt

ram A male sheep

ramekin, ramequin A small baking dish

ranch A large farm where cattle or sheep are raised

rawhide Animal skin that has not been made into leather

Red River cart A wooden handcart built without nails or other metal parts

reel A lively twirling dance

reflector oven A three-sided, metal box that held meat for cooking. The open side of the box faced the fire, and the box trapped the heat.

reservation An area of land set aside by the government, on which Native Americans live

river driver A logger who kept logs moving down the river to the sawmill

rolling pin A cylinder, usually wooden, that is used to flatten bread or pastry dough

roof tree A small tree or branch that was attached to the rafters of a new barn for good luck

root cellar A storage area dug under a house or into a hillside, used for keeping produce cool

rotary saw A round saw that cuts logs into planks in a sawmill

rug beater A fanlike object used to beat the dust and dirt from rugs and carpets

ruggle A wooden brace that stopped a wagon wheel from rolling

rustler A person who steals livestock such as cattle

ruggle

saddle A leather seat strapped to the back of a horse

saddlebag A small leather bag tied onto a saddle and used for carrying items while on horseback

salon *see* parlor

saloon A place where people gather to buy and drink alcohol; a tavern

sampler A piece of cloth embroidered with different stitches for the purpose of practicing sewing skills

sawmill A building where logs are sawed into planks

sawyer (1) A person who saws logs into planks; (2) A person who operates a sawmill

scarecrow A human-like figure made of wood and straw and placed in a field of crops in order to scare away animals

scarificator A tool made of several blades used for scratching skin in order to draw blood

scorp A short-handled knife with a curved blade used for hollowing out bowls from hard wood

Scriptures Religious writings in a holy book such as the Bible

scuttle A metal container for carrying coal; also called a hod

scythe A tool with a curved blade and wooden handle, used for cutting down grain crops and grass

seal (1) A stamp used to indent a personalized mark to show ownership; (2) A stamp used with hot wax to close letters and packages

seamstress A woman who sews and mends clothing for money

set hammer *see* flatter

settlement A small, fairly new community or village

settler A person who clears land and builds a home in an undeveloped area

shake A handcut board or shingle used on a roof to keep out rain

shanty A roughly built shack or cabin

shavinghorse A carpenter's bench that allowed people to sit as they shaped a piece of wood

saddle

saloon

sampler

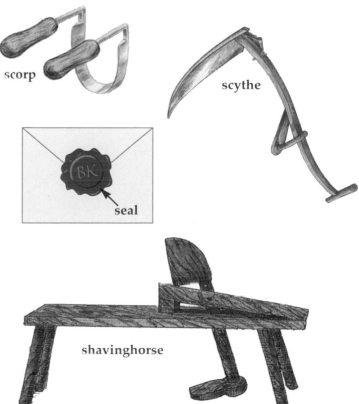
scarificator

scorp

scythe

seal

shakes

shavinghorse

shift

shuttle

shoemaker (sign)

silhouette

skein

skillet

sleigh

smock

smokehouse

soddy

shay A two- or four-wheeled carriage for two to four passengers

sheaf A bundle of hay, corn, or other grain

sheep shed A building with a roof but no wall, used for keeping sheep

shift A loose dress worn by women as underwear and a nightgown

shivaree A noisy celebration held in honor of a newly married couple; also called a charivari

shoemaker A person who makes and repairs shoes and boots

shuttle An instrument containing a spool of yarn that is passed back and forth during weaving on a loom

sickle A tool with a sharp, curved blade and a short handle, used to cut grain or grass

silhouette The shadow-like profile of a person or object filled in with black

silversmith A person who makes objects out of silver

simple A medicine made from herbs

skein A piece of thread or yarn wound in a loose coil

skillet A frying pan with a long handle

slate A small chalkboard on which schoolchildren wrote with chalk

sledge A wooden cart on runners, used to transport goods over ice

sleigh A one- or two-seated wooden cart on runners

smith A person who shapes metal, such as a blacksmith, silversmith, farrier, or founder

smock A loose-fitting shirt worn over one's clothes to protect them while working

smokehouse A small outbuilding in which meat or fish was hung up and dried over a fire to preserve it

sod A grassy strip of earth

soddy A house made from sod

soft goods *see* dry goods

sombrero A wide-brimmed Mexican hat

sheaf

sickle

slate

dog

sombrero

spice mill A tool used to grind spices such as nutmeg or peppercorns

spider A long-handled frying pan with legs, used for cooking in a fireplace

spinet A musical instrument similar to a small harpsichord

spinning wheel A machine used to make wool into yarn

spit A wooden or metal pole on which meat is turned above a fire to be cooked

spittoon A container into which people spit tobacco juice; also called a cuspidor

spree A lively gathering where people dance

springhouse A small outbuilding built over a cold-water stream, in which crocks of milk, butter, and cheese were kept cool

spur A metal gadget with a spiked wheel, worn over cowboy boots and used to urge a horse to speed up

square dance A dance in which couples form a square and follow instructions given by a caller

stable A place where horses and cows are kept

stagecoach A horse-drawn coach, or closed-in carriage, that carried people, mail, and baggage

stave A narrow, curved piece of wood used to form the side of a barrel; *see* cask

stay *see* corset

stereoscope A viewer that showed the user a three-dimensional picture

Stetson A popular type of cowboy hat

stile A set of steps used for getting over a fence

stook A collection of sheaves propped together

sugar cutter A scissor-like gadget used to cut a block or cone of sugar into smaller pieces

summer kitchen A kitchen built onto the outside of a home and used in summer so that the house would not get too hot when cooking

Sunday best Good clothes worn only to church on Sundays or on special occasions

suspenders A pair of straps worn over the shoulders to hold up a person's pants

spider

spinning wheel

spittoon

spur

spring house

stereoscope

stagecoach

Stetson

stile

stook

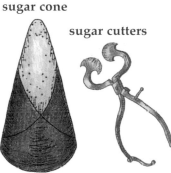

suspenders

sugar cone

sugar cutters

25

teetotum

telegraph

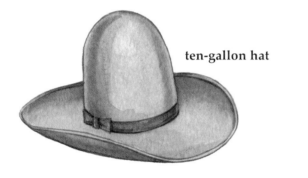

ten-gallon hat

tailor A man who sews and repairs clothing for money

tallow Melted animal fat that is used to make candles and soap

teamster (1) A person who drives a team of animals; (2) A logger who hauled logs to a river to be transported to a sawmill

teetotum A spinning top with numbers, used in games instead of dice

telegraph A system that sends long-distance messages using wire, electricity, and Morse code

ten-gallon hat A wide-brimmed, tall-crowned hat worn by a cowboy

thatch Long grasses, reeds, or straw used to cover a roof

thaumatrope A two-sided toy, each side having pictures that, when the toy is spun, appear together as a single picture

tin closet *see* pie safe

tinder Any material, such as shredded rags or wood shavings, that easily catches fire

tinderbox A small, metal box used for holding tinder and equipped with a flint and steel for making sparks to start a fire

tin lantern A tin container that holds a candle

thaumatrope

side one

side two

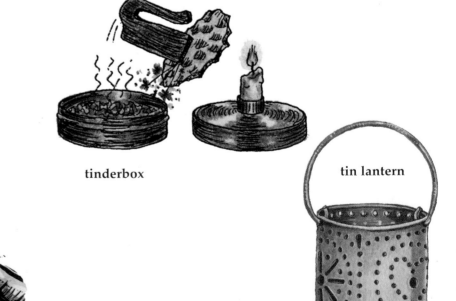

tinderbox

tin lantern

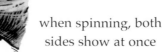

when spinning, both sides show at once

tinker A traveling mender of pots and pans

tinsmith A person who makes and repairs tin items

tire A ring, usually made of iron, that fits over the wooden rim of a wagon wheel

toasting fork A long-handled metal gadget used to toast bread over an open fire

tonic A liquid or medicine that was believed to refresh or strengthen a person

toothbrush A twig with a splintered end that pioneers used to clean their teeth

toothbrush

tradesperson A person skilled in a particular craft or trade, such as carpentry or blacksmithing

trading post A place set up by a fur-trading company at which furs were traded for supplies

trail drive An event in which cowboys guide herds of cattle from a ranch to a town to be sold

trammel A series of hooks on which pots were hung in a fireplace

trapper A person who hunts animals and sells their furs

treacle *see* molasses

tinsmith

trail drive

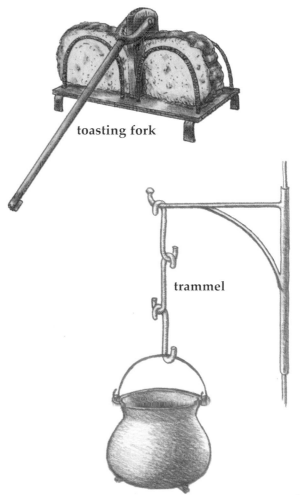

toasting fork

trammel

trencher

treenware

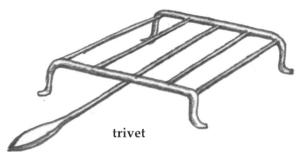

trivet

trunk

treenware Wooden household items, such as buckets, utensils, bowls, and plates

trencher A wooden dish made from a hollowed-out log, used to mix and serve food

trivet A metal stand with legs, used for supporting pots and pans over the coals of a fire

trundle bed A low bed on wheels that can be rolled under another bed when it is not in use

trunk A large storage box with a hinged lid

trussing ring A tool used by a cooper to hold the staves of a barrel together as the barrel was built

turn-up bed A bed attached to a wall at one end, and which flips up against the wall when it is not in use

type A small block with a raised letter or character on one side that is used in a printing press

type case A box full of cubby holes or compartments, each of which contained different type for the printer to use

trundle bed

type

type case

28

UV

undertaker A person who arranges funerals and prepares people who have died for burial

union suit A one-piece, men's undergarment worn for extra warmth in the winter

upholsterer A person who works at covering furniture with cushions and material

utensil Any instrument or container used in the kitchen for cooking or preparing food

valance A short decorative curtain hung across the top of a window or around the top of a canopy bed

vaquero A Spanish cowboy

varnish An oil-based liquid used to give wood a smooth, shiny finish

vegetable garden A plot of land on which vegetables are grown

velocipede An early type of bicycle or tricycle

veneer A thinly shaved sheet of wood glued onto the surface of a piece of furniture to give it a decorative finish

venison The meat of a deer

Victorian Describing the period of time between 1837 and 1901, when Queen Victoria ruled Britain; describing objects, styles, or people of this time

vigilante A person who takes the law into his or her own hands by punishing others

village A small town. Most pioneer villages had a gristmill, sawmill, general store, schoolhouse, church, inn, and shops such as a blacksmith's.

violin A stringed musical instrument that is played with a bow

undertaker (shop)

utensils

union suit

velocipede

valance

Victorian house

vaquero

violin

village

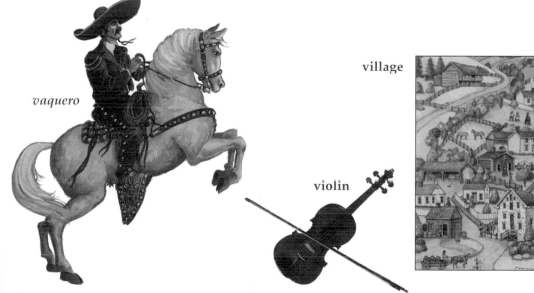

29

wagon train

wainwright (shop)

walking wheel

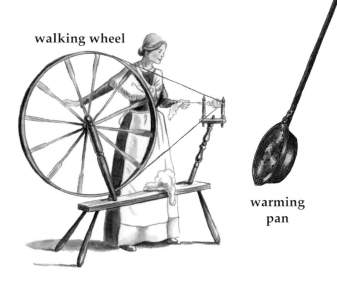

warming pan

wagon train A group of covered wagons in which many settlers traveled to the West

wainwright A person who built and repaired wagons, carriages, and sleighs

walking wheel A large spinning wheel that required the spinner to walk back and forth while spinning; also called a monster wheel

warming pan A long-handled metal pan filled with hot coals that was run across a bed to warm the sheets and covers

washboard A grooved board on which clothes were scrubbed with soap and water

washstand A cabinet or table used to hold a pitcher and basin

water wheel A large wooden wheel turned by water, which was used to power a mill

weather vane A wooden or metal object that is moved by the wind and shows the direction in which the wind is blowing

well A deep hole dug into the ground in which water from an underground source collects

whale-oil lamp A lamp fueled by whale oil, usually with two wicks

water wheel

weather vane

washstand

washboard

well

whale-oil lamp

wheelwright A person who makes wheels for wagons, carriages, and carts

whey The watery part of the milk that remains after curd has formed during the making of cheese

whipsaw A large, two-person saw used to hand-cut logs into planks

whirligig A spinning toy made from a length of string threaded through a hole in a round piece of wood

whitewash A white mixture of lime and water used to paint walls and fences

wick A loosely woven cord that draws up fuel to a flame in a candle or lamp

windmill A wooden tower with a round fanlike wheel at the top that is turned by the wind and used to power a water pump

winnowing tray A tray used to separate grain from chaff. Grain was put in the tray and then tossed into the air. The light chaff blew away in the wind, and the heavy grain fell to the floor.

wood stove An iron stove heated by a wood fire, which pioneers used for cooking

wool (1) The hair of a sheep or goat; (2) Cloth made of sheep or goat hair

woolies Chaps with fur or goat hair on the front, worn by cowboys for extra warmth

workhorse A large horse used for hard work such as pulling a plow or heavy wagon; also called a draft horse

wrought iron Iron that has been forged, or shaped, on an anvil

wheelwright
(made wheels)

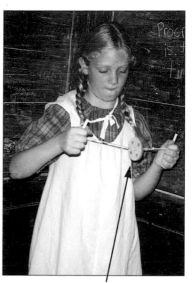

whirligig

← wick

winnowing
tray

wood stove

woolies →

wrought iron

Xmas An early way of writing the word Christmas

xylograph A picture made from a woodcut

yard goods Cloth that is sold by length

yarn A piece of twisted thread, usually made of wool, used in knitting and weaving

yeast A substance that helps bread to rise

yoke A wooden bar that fits across a person's or animal's shoulders, used to carry heavy loads

zigzag fence A fence built out of wooden rails stacked on an angle; also called a "snake" or "worm" fence

zither A musical instrument that is made up of a shallow box with 30 to 45 strings stretched over it

zoetrope A spinning toy that makes pictures appear as though they are moving

zouave jacket A short, collarless boy's jacket

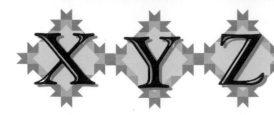

Xmas

xylograph

yard goods

yoke

zigzag fence

zither

zoetrope

zouave jacket

1 2 3 4 5 6 7 8 9 0 Printed in the U.S.A. 8 7 6 5 4 3 2 1 0 9